A
FAMILY HAGGADAH

For Families With Young Children

Shoshana Silberman

Illustrated by
Katherine Janus Kahn

KAR-BEN
PUBLISHING

To my beloved Grandma Jenny ᶻ″ˡ, whose wonderful seders made Pesach the favorite holiday of my childhood . . . and whose inspiration helps to make my own seders special.

To my editors, Judye Groner and Madeline Wikler, who gave this Haggadah generous time, abounding energy, and expert guidance . . . and to Rabbi Oscar Groner ᶻ″ˡ, for his insights and excellent suggestions.

To my children, Shmuel, Lisa, and Gabriel, whose enthusiasm encourages me to persevere, and whose devotion and love sustain me daily.

* * *

Since the first printing of *A Family Haggadah I*, our family has been joined by a son-in-law, Daniel S. Brenner, and a daughter-in-law Sarah L. Silberman, as well as six grandchildren – Noam, Jonah, Yaakov, Adira, Meir, and Chana. Each in their own way have brought much joy and Nachas.

This Haggadah is lovingly dedicated to all these dear ones, but especially to my late husband Mel, whose advice and support meant so much to me. He was an amazing person and truly an *ezer k'negdi*, a soulmate in every sense of the word. May his memory forever be a blessing.

Texts copyright © 1987 by Shoshana Silberman
Illustrations copyright © 1987 by Katherine Janus Kahn
Text and art revised 2011

KAR-BEN PUBLISHING
A division of Lerner Publishing Group, Inc.
241 FirstAvenue North
Minneapolis, MN 55401 USA
1-800-4KARBEN

Website Address: www.karben.com

Library of Congress Cataloging-in-Publication Data

Haggadah (Silberman). English & Hebrew.
　　A family Haggadah / by Shoshana Silberman ; illustrated by Katherine Janus Kahn.—
Rev. ed.
　　　　p.　cm.
　　"The seder service with English and Hebrew texts and prayers, and gender–sensitive translations, is provided on the right–hand pages. Commentaries and discussion questions are on the left–hand pages"—Data view.
　　　　ISBN 978–0–7613–5210–5 (pbk. : alk. paper)
　　　　ISBN 978–1–4677–0347–5 (eBook)
　　　　1. Haggadot—Texts. 2. Seder—Liturgy—Texts. 3. Judaism—Liturgy—Texts. 4. Haggadah.
I. Silberman, Shoshana. II. Kahn, Katherine. III. Title.
BM674.75.S55 2011
296.4'5371—dc22　　　　　　　　　　　　　　　　　　　　　　　　　　2010012733

Manufactured in the United States of America
5 — CG — 11/1/14

A NOTE TO PARENTS

For many years, parents of young children have asked me to suggest a Haggadah they could use at a family seder. Although at the time I could recommend some lovely story and activity books, there were no Haggadot specifically designed to encourage the active participation of everyone at the seder. Hence the idea for this family Haggadah was born. Its first printing was in 1987, and it has been reprinted annually ever since. Clearly it has filled a need and stood the test of time.

The format of *A Family Haggadah* is designed to enable every participant to follow along easily. The English is gender neutral and within the grasp of school-age children. The seder service is on the right-hand pages. Essential Hebrew texts are provided, with transliterations and simple translations. Discussion questions and activities are on left-hand pages. These provide the basis for exploring the rich variety of thought and insight into the text.

Do not attempt to discuss all the questions and do all the suggested activities. That would make the seder long and tedious. Leave some things over for the second seder, if you have one, and for years to come. Parents (and perhaps children) should read through the book beforehand and choose activities that are engaging and age-appropriate. Activities for very young children, and those which require advance preparation, are noted with symbols (see below). You may wish to have a seder leader, but do give each person a chance to read, and encourage everyone to join in the songs and prayers. It helps to assign children their parts in advance, so they can learn to read them aloud smoothly.

According to tradition, it is our responsibility to tell the story of the Exodus to our children, making sure that it is understood. We want them to ask questions, to challenge us and the text, and to learn in the process. For this story must become their story. They must understand its message, so that they, too, will pass it on from generation to generation.

—S.S.

*

 For young children

 Plan ahead activity

 Song

PREPARING FOR THE SEDER

In traditional Jewish homes, an elaborate spring cleaning begins weeks before Passover. This is because we are not permitted to eat or even possess food that is categorized as *chametz* (containing a leavening agent) during the holiday. For guidance on preparing your home and your kitchen, and serving permissible foods, contact your rabbi. You may also consult the many internet sites that offer information.

The evening before the first seder, it is traditional to search the house for chametz. Before the search (called *bedikat chametz*) you may wish to have a popcorn party, followed by a thorough sweep-up. It's a fun way to dramatize the last "farewell to chametz." The blessings we recite when we search for, and burn the remaining chametz the next morning, are available on the internet and in many Haggadahs.

To make the holiday important to children, involve them in the preparations. This includes cleaning their own rooms, helping to prepare the kitchen, and shopping (a wonderful opportunity to learn what is kosher for Passover and what is not). Junior cooks may be called on to make charoset, matzah balls, and Passover desserts.

Find out what songs and stories your youngsters have learned in nursery or religious school, and plan to include them in the seder. Children will be honored if you use their handmade seder plates or matzah covers.

It is customary to invite guests to the seder, and in the spirit of the holiday you may wish to include a newcomer to the community, a college student far from home, or a guest from a nursing home. Family and friends make the experience more joyful and add wisdom (and often new traditions) to the telling of the Passover story.

Passover is a time to remember those who do not share our freedom and our bounty. Many families donate their chametz to organizations that distribute food to needy non-Jews. It is also a mitzvah to make a donation to a *Ma'ot Hittim* fund. The term means "wheat money," and refers to an organization that provides Passover foods to the poor. Your rabbi or educational director can provide names and addresses of appropriate organizations to help you fulfill this mitzvah.[1]

PLATE

BEITZAH	Roasted egg*	בֵּיצָה
KARPAS	Parsley, celery, potato	כַּרְפַּס
Z'ROA	Roasted bone*	זְרוֹעַ
CHAROSET	Chopped apples and nuts	חֲרֹסֶת
MAROR	Bitter herb (whole or grated horseradish or romaine lettuce)	מָרוֹר
CHAZERET	Second bitter herb for Hillel sandwich	חֲזֶרֶת

*Vegetarians may wish to substitute an avocado seed and beet instead.

Optional:

Matzah of Hope

Afikomen Bag

Flowers

Individual seder plates with
 karpas, maror, charoset

Empty plate to remember the
 homeless

An orange as a symbol of
 inclusivity[2]

A dish of olives as a symbol of
 peace

6

SEDER CHECKLIST

Holiday candles
Wine or grape juice
Seder Plate
Cup for Elijah
Cup for Miriam
Three matzot, covered
Pillows(s) for reclining
Salt water for dipping
Cup, basin, towel for washing
Haggadah for each person
Wine cup for each person

WE LIGHT THE CANDLES

Before sunset, light candles and say this blessing:
(On Shabbat, add the words in brackets)

בָּרוּךְ אַתָּה יְיָ אֱלֹהֵינוּ מֶלֶךְ הָעוֹלָם אֲשֶׁר קִדְּשָׁנוּ בְּמִצְוֹתָיו וְצִוָּנוּ לְהַדְלִיק נֵר שֶׁל (שַׁבָּת וְשֶׁל) יוֹם טוֹב.

Baruch Atah Adonai Eloheinu melech ha'olam, asher kid'shanu b'mitzvotav v'tzivanu l'hadlik ner shel [Shabbat v'shel] Yom Tov.

We praise You, Adonai our God, Ruler of the Universe, Who makes us holy by Your mitzvot and commands us to light the [Sabbath and] festival lights.

בָּרוּךְ אַתָּה יְיָ אֱלֹהֵינוּ מֶלֶךְ הָעוֹלָם שֶׁהֶחֱיָנוּ וְקִיְּמָנוּ וְהִגִּיעָנוּ לַזְּמַן הַזֶּה.

Baruch Atah Adonai Eloheinu melech ha'olam, shehecheyanu v'kiy'manu v'higianu lazman hazeh.

We praise You, Adonai our God, Ruler of the Universe, Who has kept us alive and well so that we can celebrate this special time.

Share a holiday wish for everyone at the seder.

 Think of other occasions when candles are lit, such as Shabbat and birthdays. How do these occasions make you feel?

9

THE SEDER HAS A SPECIAL ORDER

SEDER means order. Here is the SEDER of the SEDER:

KADDESH	We say the Kiddush First cup of wine	קַדֵּשׁ
UR'CHATZ	We wash our hands	וּרְחַץ
KARPAS	We dip a vegetable in salt water and say a blessing	כַּרְפַּס
YACHATZ	We break the middle matzah and hide the larger piece, the Afikomen	יַחַץ
MAGGID	We tell the story of Passover Four Questions Second cup of wine	מַגִּיד
RACHTZAH	We wash our hands and say the blessing	רָחְצָה
MOTZI/ MATZAH	We say the blessings for "bread" and matzah	מוֹצִיא מַצָּה
MAROR	We dip the bitter herbs in charoset and say the blessing	מָרוֹר
KORECH	We eat a sandwich of matzah and bitter herbs	כּוֹרֵךְ
SHULCHAN ORECH	We eat the festive meal	שֻׁלְחָן עוֹרֵךְ
TZAFUN	We eat the Afikomen	צָפוּן
BARECH	We say the blessing after the meal Third cup of wine Welcome Elijah and Miriam	בָּרֵךְ
HALLEL	We sing songs of praise Fourth cup of wine	הַלֵּל
NIRTZAH	We complete the seder	נִרְצָה

Discuss how our world follows a seder—an order. What has an order that we might not want to be disturbed, such as a baseball game or a symphony?

 Describe a backwards or "topsy-turvy" day. (I go to school, and then I get dressed.)

The seder is done today as it has been done for 2,000 years. What feels good about that?

 If you know the melody, sing the "Seder of the Seder (Kaddesh Ur'chatz)." Try adding hand motions as you sing. Before you begin each new part of the seder, sing the song again—just to that part.

As the seder begins, complete this sentence: "At this seder, I hope…"

WE SAY THE KIDDUSH

THE FIRST CUP

(Fill cups with wine or grape juice)

We lift our cups to say the blessing over the first cup of wine:

(On Shabbat, add the words in brackets)

[וַיְהִי־עֶרֶב וַיְהִי־בֹקֶר יוֹם הַשִּׁשִּׁי.
וַיְכֻלּוּ הַשָּׁמַיִם וְהָאָרֶץ וְכָל־צְבָאָם. וַיְכַל אֱלֹהִים בַּיּוֹם הַשְּׁבִיעִי מְלַאכְתּוֹ
אֲשֶׁר עָשָׂה, וַיִּשְׁבֹּת בַּיּוֹם הַשְּׁבִיעִי מִכָּל־מְלַאכְתּוֹ אֲשֶׁר עָשָׂה. וַיְבָרֶךְ
אֱלֹהִים אֶת־יוֹם הַשְּׁבִיעִי וַיְקַדֵּשׁ אֹתוֹ, כִּי בוֹ שָׁבַת מִכָּל־מְלַאכְתּוֹ אֲשֶׁר
בָּרָא אֱלֹהִים לַעֲשׂוֹת.]

*[Vay'hi erev vay'hi voker yom hashishi. Vay'chulu hashamayim v'ha'aretz
v'chol tsz'va'am. Vay'chal Elohim bayom hash'vi'i m'lachto asher asah.
Vayishbot bayom hash'vi'i mikol m'lachto asher asah. Vay'varech Elohim et
yom hash'vi'i vay'kadesh oto, ki vo shavat mikol m'lachto asher bara Elohim
la'asot.]*

[On the sixth day, the heavens and the earth were completed. On the seventh day, God finished the work of creation and rested. God blessed the seventh day and called it holy, because on that day God rested from the work of creation.]

בָּרוּךְ אַתָּה יְיָ אֱלֹהֵינוּ מֶלֶךְ הָעוֹלָם בּוֹרֵא פְּרִי הַגָּפֶן.

Baruch Atah Adonai Eloheinu melech ha'olam, borei p'ri hagafen.

We praise You, Adonai our God, Ruler of the Universe, Who creates the fruit of the vine.

The seder Kiddush says that Pesach cele-
brates our leaving Egypt. The Kiddush we
recite on Shabbat contains these exact same
words. How is Shabbat also a celebration of
freedom?

 Kiddush countdown: Before the seder, make
cup counters. Draw four wine cups on con-
struction paper, and cut them out. Number
the cups one to four. At the appropriate time,
children may hold them up to show which
cup of wine is being blessed.

בָּרוּךְ אַתָּה יְיָ אֱלֹהֵינוּ מֶלֶךְ הָעוֹלָם אֲשֶׁר בָּחַר בָּנוּ מִכָּל־עָם וְרוֹמְמָנוּ מִכָּל־לָשׁוֹן וְקִדְּשָׁנוּ בְּמִצְוֹתָיו. וַתִּתֶּן־לָנוּ יְיָ אֱלֹהֵינוּ בְּאַהֲבָה (שַׁבָּתוֹת לִמְנוּחָה וּ)מוֹעֲדִים לְשִׂמְחָה חַגִּים וּזְמַנִּים לְשָׂשׂוֹן אֶת־יוֹם (הַשַּׁבָּת הַזֶּה וְאֶת־יוֹם) חַג הַמַּצּוֹת הַזֶּה, זְמַן חֵרוּתֵנוּ, (בְּאַהֲבָה) מִקְרָא קֹדֶשׁ זֵכֶר לִיצִיאַת מִצְרָיִם. כִּי בָנוּ בָחַרְתָּ וְאוֹתָנוּ קִדַּשְׁתָּ מִכָּל־הָעַמִּים (וְשַׁבָּת) וּמוֹעֲדֵי קָדְשֶׁךָ (בְּאַהֲבָה וּבְרָצוֹן) בְּשִׂמְחָה וּבְשָׂשׂוֹן הִנְחַלְתָּנוּ. בָּרוּךְ אַתָּה יְיָ מְקַדֵּשׁ (הַשַּׁבָּת וְ)יִשְׂרָאֵל וְהַזְּמַנִּים.

Baruch Atah Adonai Eloheinu melech ha'olam, asher bachar banu mikol am. V'rom'manu mikol lashon, v'kid'shanu b'mitzvotav. Vatiten lanu Adonai Eloheinu b'ahavah [Shabbatot lim'nuchah u'] mo'adim l'simchah chagim uz'manim l'sasson. Et yom [haShabbat hazeh v'et yom] chag hamatzot hazeh z'man cherutenu [b'ahavah] mikra kodesh zecher liy'tziat Mitzrayim. Ki vanu vacharta v'otanu kidashta mikol ha'amin [v'Shabbat] u'moadei kadsh'cha [b'ahavah] uv'ratzon b'simchah u'v'sasson hinchaltanu. Baruch Atah Adonai mikadesh [haShabbat v'] Yisrael v'hazmanim.

We praise You, Adonai our God, Ruler of the Universe, Who has made us holy through your mitzvot and loving-ly given us [Shabbat for rest and] festivals for gladness. You have given us (Shabbat and) this Festival of Matzot, celebrations of our freedom, a holy time to recall our go-ing out of Egypt. We praise You Adonai, Who makes holy [Shabbat] the people Israel, and the festivals.

◄ *On Saturday night, add Havdallah (on facing page)* ►

בָּרוּךְ אַתָּה יְיָ אֱלֹהֵינוּ מֶלֶךְ הָעוֹלָם שֶׁהֶחֱיָנוּ וְקִיְּמָנוּ וְהִגִּיעָנוּ לַזְּמַן הַזֶּה.

Baruch Atah Adonai, Eloheinu melech ha'olam shehecheyanu, v'kiy'manu, v'higianu, lazman hazeh.

We praise you, Adonai our God, Ruler of the Universe, Who has kept us alive and well so that we can celebrate this special time.

(All drink the wine or grape juice)

HAVDALLAH

בָּרוּךְ אַתָּה יְיָ אֱלֹהֵינוּ מֶלֶךְ הָעוֹלָם בּוֹרֵא מְאוֹרֵי הָאֵשׁ.

Baruch Atah Adonai Eloheinu melech ha'olam, borei m'orei ha'esh.

We praise you, Adonai our God, Ruler of the Universe, Creator of light.

בָּרוּךְ אַתָּה יְיָ אֱלֹהֵינוּ מֶלֶךְ הָעוֹלָם הַמַּבְדִּיל בֵּין קֹדֶשׁ לְחֹל, בֵּין אוֹר לְחֹשֶׁךְ, בֵּין יִשְׂרָאֵל לָעַמִּים, בֵּין יוֹם הַשְּׁבִיעִי לְשֵׁשֶׁת יְמֵי הַמַּעֲשֶׂה. בֵּין קְדֻשַּׁת שַׁבָּת לִקְדֻשַּׁת יוֹם טוֹב הִבְדַּלְתָּ, וְאֶת־יוֹם הַשְּׁבִיעִי מִשֵּׁשֶׁת יְמֵי הַמַּעֲשֶׂה קִדַּשְׁתָּ, הִבְדַּלְתָּ וְקִדַּשְׁתָּ אֶת־עַמְּךָ יִשְׂרָאֵל בִּקְדֻשָּׁתֶךָ. בָּרוּךְ אַתָּה יְיָ הַמַּבְדִּיל בֵּין קֹדֶשׁ לְקֹדֶשׁ.

Baruch Atah Adonai hamavdil bein kodesh l'kodesh.

We praise you Adonai our God, Ruler of the Universe, Who separates holy from not holy, light from darkness, Israel from the nations, and Shabbat from the six days of creation. We praise You, Adonai, Who separates the holiness of Shabbat from the holiness of the festivals.

Continue with Shehecheyanu (opposite) ▶

The celebration of Pesach extends the spirit of Shabbat, so we do not recite the blessing over the spices. The blessing for light is said over the holiday candles and not over a Havdallah candle.

WE WASH OUR HANDS

(Take a cup or pitcher of water in one hand and pour it over the other hand. Then do the same, reversing hands. This can be done at a sink, or with a cup and basin at the table. No blessing is recited.)

WE DIP A VEGETABLE

(Give everyone a green vegetable)

We dip a vegetable into salt water and say this blessing:

בָּרוּךְ אַתָּה יְיָ אֱלֹהֵינוּ מֶלֶךְ הָעוֹלָם בּוֹרֵא פְּרִי הָאֲדָמָה.

Baruch Atah Adonai Eloheinu melech ha'olam, borei p'ri ha'adamah.

We praise You, Adonai our God, Ruler of the Universe, Who creates the fruit of the earth.

(All eat the vegetable)

As an act of purification, the *kohanim*, priests of old, washed their hands before doing rituals and blessing the people. Washing our hands helps us feel "Pesach-dik" and ready for the seder. How did you get ready for the seder? How did you help prepare your home for Passover?

Talk about how athletes warm up or how actors get ready to go on stage.

DODI LI

On Pesach we read from the *Song of Songs*. Its poetry of nature and of love recalls God's covenant with the people of Israel.

דּוֹדִי לִי וַאֲנִי לוֹ
הָרוֹעֶה בַּשׁוֹשַׁנִּים.

מִי זֹאת עוֹלָה מִן הַמִּדְבָּר
מְקֻטֶּרֶת מוֹר וּלְבוֹנָה.

Dodi li va'ani lo, haro'eh bashoshanim.
Mi zot olah min hamidbar, m'kuteret mor ul'vonah.

My beloved is mine and I am his, who browses among the lilies. Who is she coming from the desert, in clouds of myrrh and frankincense?

Karpas is a symbol of spring and of renewal. How many signs of spring can you think of?

The salt water reminds us of the tears our ancestors shed in Egypt. What happened to the slaves to make them cry?

Put a fresh flower at each place setting, so everyone can smell the fragrance of spring.

Karpas was served as an appetizer at festive meals in ancient times. Serving vegetable hors d'oeuvres and a dip at this point in the seder will help hungry children (and adults) hold out until the meal is served.[3]

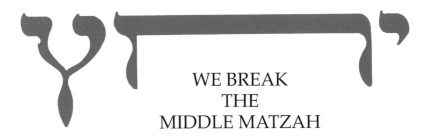

WE BREAK
THE
MIDDLE MATZAH

We break the middle matzah into two pieces. We wrap and set aside the larger piece as the Afikomen, the dessert matzah to be eaten after the meal. The smaller piece is returned to its place.

(Uncover the plate of matzah and raise it for all to see)

הָא לַחְמָא עַנְיָא דִּי אֲכַלוּ אַבְהָתַנָא בְּאַרְעָא דְמִצְרָיִם.
כָּל־דִכְפִין יֵיתֵי וְיֵכֹל, כָּל־דִצְרִיךְ יֵיתֵי וְיִפְסַח. הָשַׁתָּא הָכָא,
לְשָׁנָה הַבָּאָה בְּאַרְעָא דְיִשְׂרָאֵל. הָשַׁתָּא עַבְדֵי, לְשָׁנָה הַבָּאָה
בְּנֵי חוֹרִין.

Halachma Anya di achalu ahavatana b'ara d'Mitzrayim. Kol dichfin yeitei v'yechol. Kol ditzrich yetei v'yifsach. Hashata hacha lashanah haba'ah b'ara d'Yisrael. Hashata avdei lashanah haba'ah b'nei chorin.

This is the bread of poverty which our ancestors ate in the land of Egypt. All who are hungry, come and eat. All who are needy, come and celebrate Passover with us. Now we celebrate here. Next year may we be in the land of Israel. Now we are slaves. Next year may we be truly free.

(Fill the wine cups for the second time)

THE MATZAH OF HOPE

(Lift the designated matzah ad set it aside)

We set aside this matzah as a symbol of hope for all those in the world who are in despair. Some are crushed by poverty and disease, others by tyranny and violence. We pray that their pain will end soon, and they will be brought to safety and healing. We dedicate ourselves to relieve suffering in whatever form it takes.

 Matzah is known as the "bread of poverty." One reason we break the middle matzah is to show that the poor need to set aside some of their food for the next meal. What can we set aside to share with someone less fortunate? [4]

Some say the middle matzah is broken because our redemption is not complete. What is incomplete in our world? What problems do you wish we could solve?

Afikomen is a Greek word meaning dessert. The reading *Halachma Anya*, (this is the bread of poverty) is in Aramaic. These languages were spoken by Jews during the time when the Haggadah was written. What languages do Jews speak today?

 It's time for Afikomen hiding games! In some families, the seder leader hides the Afikomen when the children are not looking. The child who finds it later on (or all the children) win(s) a prize. In other families, children "steal" the Afikomen during the seder and hide it. After the meal, the leader must find it, or offer a reward for its return.

WE TELL THE STORY OF PASSOVER

THE FOUR QUESTIONS

מַה־נִּשְׁתַּנָּה הַלַּיְלָה הַזֶּה מִכָּל־הַלֵּילוֹת!

Mah nishtanah halailah hazeh mikol haleilot!

How different this night is from all other nights!

1

On all other nights we eat bread or matzah.
On this night why do we eat only matzah?

2

On all other nights we eat all kinds of vegetables.
On this night why do we eat only maror?

3

On all other nights we do not have to dip vegetables even once. On this night why do we dip them twice?

4

On all other nights we eat our meals sitting any way we like. On this night why do we lean on pillows?

THE FOUR QUESTIONS

מַה־נִּשְׁתַּנָּה הַלַּיְלָה הַזֶּה מִכָּל־הַלֵּילוֹת!

שֶׁבְּכָל־הַלֵּילוֹת אָנוּ אוֹכְלִין חָמֵץ וּמַצָּה,
הַלַּיְלָה הַזֶּה כֻּלּוֹ מַצָּה.

שֶׁבְּכָל־הַלֵּילוֹת אָנוּ אוֹכְלִין שְׁאָר יְרָקוֹת,
הַלַּיְלָה הַזֶּה מָרוֹר.

שֶׁבְּכָל־הַלֵּילוֹת אֵין אָנוּ מַטְבִּילִין אֲפִלּוּ
פַּעַם אֶחָת, הַלַּיְלָה הַזֶּה שְׁתֵּי פְעָמִים.

שֶׁבְּכָל־הַלֵּילוֹת אָנוּ אוֹכְלִין בֵּין יוֹשְׁבִין וּבֵין
מְסֻבִּין, הַלַּיְלָה הַזֶּה כֻּלָּנוּ מְסֻבִּין.

Mah nishtanah halailah hazeh mikol haleilot!

Sheb'chol haleilot anu ochlin chametz u'matzah.
Halailah hazeh kulo matzah.

Sheb'chol haleilot anu ochlin she'ar yirakot.
Halailah hazeh maror.

Sheb'chol haleilot ein anu matbilin afilu pa'am
echat. Halailah hazeh sh'tei f'amim.

Sheb'chol haleilot anu ochlin bein yoshvin u'vein
m'subin. Halailah hazeh kulanu m'subin.

FOUR MORE QUESTIONS

1. Why do we have to ask the same Four Questions year after year?

2. Why does the youngest child ask the Four Questions?

3. What other questions can you ask about the seder?

4. Where else does the number four appear in the seder?

WE BEGIN TO ANSWER

עֲבָדִים הָיִינוּ לְפַרְעֹה בְּמִצְרָיִם. וַיּוֹצִיאֵנוּ יְיָ אֱלֹהֵינוּ מִשָּׁם בְּיָד חֲזָקָה וּבִזְרוֹעַ נְטוּיָה. וְאִלּוּ לֹא הוֹצִיא הַקָּדוֹשׁ בָּרוּךְ הוּא אֶת־אֲבוֹתֵינוּ מִמִּצְרַיִם, הֲרֵי אָנוּ וּבָנֵינוּ וּבְנֵי בָנֵינוּ מְשֻׁעְבָּדִים הָיִינוּ לְפַרְעֹה בְּמִצְרָיִם. וַאֲפִלּוּ כֻּלָּנוּ חֲכָמִים, כֻּלָּנוּ נְבוֹנִים, כֻּלָּנוּ זְקֵנִים, כֻּלָּנוּ יוֹדְעִים אֶת־הַתּוֹרָה, מִצְוָה עָלֵינוּ לְסַפֵּר בִּיצִיאַת מִצְרָיִם. וְכָל־הַמַּרְבֶּה לְסַפֵּר בִּיצִיאַת מִצְרַיִם הֲרֵי זֶה מְשֻׁבָּח.

Avadim hayinu l'Pharaoh b'Mitzrayim.

This night is different from all the other nights because once we were slaves to Pharaoh in Egypt, but Adonai, our God, took us out with a mighty hand and an outstretched arm. If Adonai had not brought our ancestors out of Egypt, then we, and our children, and our children's children would still be slaves in the land of Egypt. Even if we know the story well and have told it many times, the more we tell it in great detail, the more we are to be praised.

This night is also different because once we worshipped idols, but now we worship only Adonai, the One Who Is Everywhere.

בָּרוּךְ הַמָּקוֹם, בָּרוּךְ הוּא.
בָּרוּךְ שֶׁנָּתַן תּוֹרָה לְעַמּוֹ יִשְׂרָאֵל, בָּרוּךְ הוּא.

Baruch HaMakom, Baruch Hu.
Baruch shenatan Torah l'amo Yisrael, Baruch Hu.

Praised be God Who Is Everywhere. Praised be God. Praised be God who gave the Torah to the people of Israel. Praised be God.

AVADIM HAYINU

Avadim hayinu; atah b'nai chorin.
Once we were slaves, but now we are free.

 LET MY PEOPLE GO

When Israel was in Egypt land.
Let my people go.
Oppressed so hard they could not stand.
Let my people go.
Go down, Moses, way down in Egypt land.
Tell ol' Pharaoh to let my people go.

"Thus saith the Lord," bold Moses said.
"Let my people go.
"If not I'll smite your first-born dead.
"Let my people go."
Go down, Moses, way down in Egypt land.
Tell ol' Pharaoh to let my people go.

The Talmud says that when we tell the story of Pesach, we should begin with despair and end with joy. The Haggadah does this in two ways. The first begins with the idea that our people were slaves to Pharaoh in Egypt, and God brought them to freedom. The second begins with the idea that our ancestors were idol-worshippers, and now we worship only God. Why does the Haggadah talk about both physical and spiritual slavery?

What kinds of things are we free to do in our country that many people around the world are not free to do?

 Bukharian Jews have an interesting custom. When they come to "Avadim hayinu—we were slaves in Egypt," the leader of the seder stands up and walks around in a bent-over position as if he or she were a slave. You can do this, too.[5]

THE FOUR CHILDREN

The Torah commands us to teach our children about Passover. The Talmud suggests four different ways children might react.

The WISE child might ask: ▬▬▬▬▬▬▬▬▬▬▬▬▬▬▬

What is the meaning of the laws and rules which Adonai our God has commanded us?

We should explain to this child in great detail all the laws and customs of Passover.

The WICKED child might ask: ▬▬▬▬▬▬▬▬▬▬▬▬▬

What does this service mean to you?

Since this child does not want to be included in the celebration, we must answer harshly: "We celebrate Passover because of what Adonai did for us. If you had been in Egypt, you would not have been included when Adonai freed us from slavery."

The SIMPLE child might ask: ▬▬▬▬▬▬▬▬▬▬▬▬▬

What is this all about?

We answer simply that, "With a mighty hand Adonai took us out of Egypt."

What about the child who DOESN'T KNOW ENOUGH TO ASK A QUESTION? ▬▬▬▬▬▬▬▬▬▬

We must explain to this child that we observe Passover to remember what God did for us when we were freed from slavery in Egypt.

How would *you* explain Passover to each of the four children?

 What job would you give each of them to help get ready for the seder?

There is a little of the four children in each of us. Describe situations where you felt wise, wicked, simple, or didn't know what to ask.[6]

What other kinds of children can you describe? How would you explain Passover to them?

THE PASSOVER STORY

God promised Abraham and Sarah that their children would become a great people. God made this promise again to each new generation—to Isaac and Rebecca, and to Jacob, Rachel, and Leah.

One of Jacob's sons, Joseph, came to live in the land of Egypt and was an advisor to the Pharaoh. He told Pharaoh to build storehouses and fill them with grain. When years of famine struck, there was food to eat in Egypt. The Pharaoh was so grateful that when Joseph's brothers came in search of food, he invited them to settle. They lived there in peace for many years and became known as the Israelites.

Years later, a new Pharaoh came to rule who did not remember Joseph and all he had done for the Egyptian people. He only feared that the Israelites would become too numerous and too powerful.

SLAVERY IN EGYPT

This Pharaoh made the Israelites slaves. He forced them to do hard labor, building cities with bricks made from clay and straw. The people knew neither peace nor rest, only misery and pain. The cruelest decree of all was the Pharaoh's order that every baby boy born to an Israelite woman be drowned in the River Nile.

One couple, Amram and Yocheved, would not kill their newborn son. Instead, they hid him in their hut for three months. When his cries became too loud, Yocheved placed him in a basket on the river. Their daughter Miriam watched to see what would happen.

The Passover story was originally told orally by parents to their children. You may wish to skip over this section and tell the story in other ways. Here are some suggestions:

- Tell the story in your own words. One volunteer may begin and others may continue.

- Pantomime the story as it is being told or read.

- Assign participants parts of the story ahead of time. They may wish to prepare a puppet show, or other creative way of telling their parts. [7]

- Invite children to share Haggadot they have made in school.

- Select a volunteer "talk show host" to interview important persons in the story. Choose others to be Moses, Yocheved, Miriam or even funny, made-up characters such as a frog from the ten plagues.

- Ask someone to play a reporter assigned to cover the crossing of the Red Sea. Describe what is happening.

 BUILDING CITIES ▬▬▬

Bang, bang, bang,
Hold your hammer low.
Bang, bang, bang,
Give a heavy blow.
For it's work, work, work
Every day and every night.
For it's work, work, work
When it's dark and when it's light. [8]

When the Pharaoh's daughter came to bathe in the river, she discovered the basket. She felt pity for the helpless child and decided to keep him as her own. She named him Moshe (Moses), which means "drawn from the water."

Bravely, Miriam asked the princess if she needed a nurse to help her with the baby. The princess said yes, and so it happened that Yocheved was able to care for her own son and teach him about his heritage.

MOSES GROWS UP

Moses would have lived at the Pharaoh's palace forever, but he could not ignore the suffering of his people. Once when he saw an Egyptian beating an Israelite slave, he could not control his anger, and he killed the Egyptian. Knowing his life would be in danger once the news of this deed spread, Moses fled to the land of Midian where he became a shepherd.

One day, while tending sheep on Mount Horeb, Moses saw a bush that seemed to be on fire, but was not burning up. From the bush, he heard God's voice calling him. God said "I am the God of your ancestors. I have seen the suffering of the Israelites and have heard their cries. I am ready to take them out of Egypt and bring them to a new land, a land flowing with milk and honey."

God told Moses to return to Egypt to bring the message of freedom to the Israelites and to warn Pharaoh that God would bring plagues on the Egyptians if he did not let the slaves go free. Moses was such a humble man that he could not imagine being God's messenger. "I will be with you," God promised Moses. With this assurance and challenge, Moses set out for Egypt.

If you were the casting director for the TV special of the Exodus, whom would you choose to play the part of Pharaoh? Moses as a young boy? Moses as a man? Yocheved? Miriam? What part would you like to play? Why?[9]

The Torah tells us that Moses was reluctant to be God's messenger. One reason is that he had a speech defect. Moses is assured that God will be with him and that his brother Aaron will help him. Why did God choose a leader who had a disability, a leader who was not perfect?

In many Haggadot there are no odes to, or poems about Moses. Traditional Haggadot do not even mention him. Some say this is so that we don't worship Moses as a god, but rather see the Exodus as the work of the Almighty. Others say it is so we don't come to believe that we can only accomplish our goals when there is a strong leader. Each of us must act to bring freedom and peace. Do you think that Moses should be included in the Haggadah?

A MIDRASH

When Moses was a shepherd in Midian, a little lamb wandered off from the flock. Though tired from a long day, Moses went to search for the lamb. When he finally found him, Moses gently carried the lamb back to the flock. God saw this act and knew that someone who would care for a little lamb in such a loving way would care for God's flock, the children of Israel.[10] Can you invent a "test" to judge a person for an important leadership position, such as the presidency?

THE TEN PLAGUES

When Moses asked Pharaoh to free the Israelites, he refused, so God brought ten plagues on the Egyptians. Each one frightened Pharaoh, and each time he promised to free the slaves. But when each plague ended, Pharaoh did not keep his word. It was only after the last plague, the death of the firstborn of the Egyptians, that Pharaoh agreed to let the Israelites go.

We fill our wine cups to remember our joy in being able to leave Egypt. Yet our happiness is not complete, because the Egyptians, who are also God's children, suffered from Pharaoh's evil ways. Therefore, we spill a drop of wine from our cups (with a finger or a spoon) as we say each plague:

BLOOD	*Dahm*	דָּם
FROGS	*Tz'fardaya*	צְפַרְדֵּעַ
LICE	*Kinim*	כִּנִּים
BEASTS	*Arov*	עָרוֹב
CATTLE DISEASE	*Dever*	דֶּבֶר
BOILS	*Sh'chin*	שְׁחִין
HAIL	*Barad*	בָּרָד
LOCUSTS	*Arbeh*	אַרְבֶּה
DARKNESS	*Choshech*	חֹשֶׁךְ
PLAGUE OF THE FIRSTBORN	*Makat B'chorot*	מַכַּת בְּכוֹרוֹת

  ## LISTEN KING PHARAOH

  Oh listen, Oh listen,
Oh listen, King Pharaoh.
Oh listen, Oh listen,
Please let my people go.
They want to go away,
They work too hard all day.
King Pharaoh, King Pharaoh,
What do you say?
No, no, no!
I will not let them go![11]

THE FROG SONG

*(Get up and jump around like frogs while you
    sing!)*
One morning when Pharaoh woke in his
    bed,
There were frogs on his head and frogs in
    his bed,
Frogs on his nose and frogs on his toes,
Frogs here, frogs there, frogs jumping
    everywhere![12]

When reading the Haggadah, some people
prefer to call Egypt by its Hebrew name,
Mitzrayim, to distinguish the Egypt of Pharaoh from the Egypt of today. What do you
think?

How are strikes and boycotts used like
plagues to apply pressure to bring about
change?

31

CROSSING THE SEA

Soon after Pharaoh let the Israelites leave Egypt, he regretted his decision and ordered his army to bring them back. His soldiers caught up with the Israelites by the banks of the Sea of Reeds. When they saw the Egyptians, they were afraid and cried out. Adonai told Moses to lift his staff, and when he did, a strong east wind drove back the sea, leaving space for the Israelites to go across on dry land. The Egyptians came after them into the sea.Moses again lifted his staff, and the waters rushed back, covering the Egyptians and their horses and chariots.

Then Moses' sister Miriam led the women in joyous dance and song, thanking Adonai for saving their lives.

GOD'S PROMISE

Long ago, Adonai promised Abraham and Sarah that their children would be a great people. It is this promise that has given our ancestors courage and hope.

(Raise cup while saying:)

וְהִיא שֶׁעָמְדָה לַאֲבוֹתֵינוּ וְלָנוּ. שֶׁלֹא אֶחָד בִּלְבַד עָמַד עָלֵינוּ לְכַלּוֹתֵינוּ. אֶלָּא שֶׁבְּכָל־דּוֹר וָדוֹר עוֹמְדִים עָלֵינוּ לְכַלּוֹתֵינוּ. וְהַקָּדוֹשׁ בָּרוּךְ הוּא מַצִּילֵנוּ מִיָּדָם.

Vehi she'amdah la'avotenu v'lanu. Shelo echad bilvad amad aleinu l'chalotenu. Ela sheb'chol dor vador omdim aleinu l'chalotenu. VeHakadosh Baruch Hu matzilenu miyadam.

More than once in our history, enemies have tried to destroy our people, but the Jewish people lives.

Pretend you must leave home for good. You have 24 hours to pack one small suitcase. What three things would you want to take with you? Why? [13]

Could there be a Jewish people without the experience of going out of Egypt?

 A GAME TO PLAY

Go around the table and have each person say, "I am leaving Egypt and I am taking a _____." Everyone must repeat what has been said before and add an item, going according to the alphabet. Be careful not to take anything that is not kosher for Passover! If you know Hebrew, try playing according to the Hebrew alphabet. [14]

DAYENU

Adonai has shown our people so many acts of kindness.
For each one, we say *dayenu*, meaning "that alone would
have been enough, for that alone we are grateful."

אִלּוּ הוֹצִיאָנוּ מִמִּצְרַיִם, דַּיֵּנוּ.

Ilu hotzianu miMitzrayim. Dayenu.

אִלּוּ נָתַן לָנוּ אֶת־הַשַּׁבָּת, דַּיֵּנוּ.

Ilu natan lanu et haShabbat. Dayenu.

אִלּוּ נָתַן לָנוּ אֶת־הַתּוֹרָה, דַּיֵּנוּ.

Ilu natan lanu et haTorah. Dayenu.

Adonai took us out of Egypt	DAYENU
Punished the Egyptians and destroyed their idols	DAYENU
Divided the sea and led us across on dry land	DAYENU
Took care of us in the desert for forty years and fed us manna	DAYENU
Gave us Shabbat	DAYENU
Brought us to Mount Sinai and gave us the Torah	DAYENU
Brought us to the land of Israel and built the Holy Temple	DAYENU
For all these—alone and together—we say	DAYENU!

THE PASSOVER SYMBOLS

Rabbi Gamliel said that in telling the story of the Exodus, we must explain the meaning of the three most important symbols. Without this explanation our celebration is incomplete.

| PESACH | | פסח |

(Point to the lamb bone or beet)

The roasted bone is called the Pesach (Passover). It recalls the lamb our ancestors sacrificed and ate in the days of the Temple. As a symbol on our seder plate, it reminds us that during the tenth plague, Adonai "passed over" the homes of the Israelites and spared their first born.

| MATZAH | | מצה |

(Lift up the matzah)

We eat matzah to remind us how our ancestors had to leave Egypt in such haste that the dough for their bread did not have time to rise.

| MAROR | | מרור |

(Lift up the bitter herb)

We eat this maror to remind us how bitter the Egyptians made the lives of our ancestors by forcing them to be slaves.

Rabbi Gamliel, who lived in the first century, was a great teacher and scholar. He helped formulate the Passover seder after the destruction of the Temple. Do you agree with his statement about the seder symbols, or do you think another part of the seder is more important?

 The "wise" child might enjoy reading the actual verses about each symbol from the Torah text:

Pesach: *Exodus 12:26-27*

Matzah: *Exodus 12:39*

Maror: *Exodus 1:13-14*

The three symbols all focus on courage and faith:

Pesach: The Israelites risked their lives by sacrificing an animal that was holy to the Egyptians.

Matzah: The Israelites took their unleavened bread and followed God into the desert into the unknown.

Maror: The Israelites were not defeated by slavery. They had hope in their hearts for a future of freedom.[15]

Share stories of people you have read about or have known personally who have acted courageously.

 Share a time when you were very brave.

Compose an advertisement for matzah or maror. Tell why people should try it.

IN EVERY GENERATION

בְּכָל־דּוֹר וָדוֹר חַיָּב אָדָם לִרְאוֹת אֶת־עַצְמוֹ כְּאִלּוּ הוּא יָצָא מִמִּצְרַיִם.

B'chol dor vador chayav adam lirot et atzmo k'ilo hu yatza mi'Mitzrayim.
In each generation, everyone must think of himself or herself as having personally left Egypt.

SONGS OF PRAISE

(Lift wine cups and say:)

It is our duty to give thanks, sing praises, and offer blessings to the Holy One Who did these miracles for our ancestors and for us. For bringing us:

> from slavery to freedom,
> from sadness to joy,
> from darkness to light.

וְנֹאמַר לְפָנָיו שִׁירָה חֲדָשָׁה, הַלְלוּיָה.

Venomar l'fanav shirah chadashah, Halleluyah.

Therefore, let us sing a new song, Halleluyah.

הַלְלוּיָה. הַלְלוּ עַבְדֵי יְיָ,
הַלְלוּ אֶת־שֵׁם יְיָ.
יְהִי שֵׁם יְיָ מְבֹרָךְ
מֵעַתָּה וְעַד עוֹלָם.

Halleluyah hal'lu avdei Adonai,
Hallelu et shem Adonai.
Yehi shem Adonai m'vorach
Me'atah v'ad olam.

Halleluyah.
Give praise to Adonai.
Sing praises, those who serve Adonai.
Blessed is the Name of Adonai now and forever.

 Although God is not a person with physical attributes, we often describe God in human terms to better understand God's ways. For example, to describe God's power we say that God took us out of Egypt "with a mighty hand and an outstretched arm." God is sometimes described in other terms as well. Complete these sentences:[16]

God is like a rock because . . .
God is like a pillow because . . .
God is like air because . . .
God is like . . .

בְּצֵאת יִשְׂרָאֵל מִמִּצְרָיִם   בֵּית יַעֲקֹב מֵעַם לֹעֵז.
הָיְתָה יְהוּדָה לְקָדְשׁוֹ   יִשְׂרָאֵל מַמְשְׁלוֹתָיו.
הַיָּם רָאָה וַיָּנֹס   הַיַּרְדֵּן יִסֹּב לְאָחוֹר.
הֶהָרִים רָקְדוּ כְאֵילִים   גְּבָעוֹת כִּבְנֵי־צֹאן.
מַה־לְּךָ הַיָּם, כִּי תָנוּס   הַיַּרְדֵּן תִּסֹּב לְאָחוֹר.
הֶהָרִים תִּרְקְדוּ כְאֵילִים   גְּבָעוֹת, כִּבְנֵי־צֹאן
מִלִּפְנֵי אָדוֹן חוּלִי אָרֶץ   מִלִּפְנֵי אֱלוֹהַּ יַעֲקֹב.
הַהֹפְכִי הַצּוּר אֲגַם־מָיִם   חַלָּמִישׁ לְמַעְיְנוֹ־מָיִם.

When the people of Israel left Egypt, they became God's people. The sea fled at the sight, and the river Jordan turned backwards. Mountains skipped like rams, and all of nature trembled at the presence of the Holy One.

THE SECOND CUP

(Lift wine cups and say:)

We praise You, Adonai our God, Ruler of the Universe, Who has freed us and our ancestors from Egypt and brought us here this night to eat matzah and maror. Adonai, our God and God of our ancestors, help us celebrate future holidays and festivals in peace and in joy. Then we will thank You with a new song.

בָּרוּךְ אַתָּה יְיָ גָּאַל יִשְׂרָאֵל.

Baruch Atah Adonai, ga'al Yisrael.

We praise You, Adonai our God, Who has freed the people of Israel.

בָּרוּךְ אַתָּה יְיָ, אֱלֹהֵינוּ מֶלֶךְ הָעוֹלָם בּוֹרֵא פְּרִי הַגָּפֶן.

Baruch Atah Adonai Eloheinu melech ha'olam, borei p'ri hagafen.

We praise You, Adonai our God, Ruler of the Universe, Who creates the fruit of the vine.

(Drink the second cup)

B'tzet Yisrael mi'Mitzrayim;
Bet Ya'akov me'am lo'ez.
Hay'tah Yehudah l'kadsho;
Yisrael mamsh'lotav.
Hayam ra'ah vayanos;
HaYarden yisov l'achor.
Heharim rakdu ch'eilim;
G'va'ot kiv'nei tzon.
Mah l'cha hayam ki tanus;
HaYarden tisov l'achor.
Heharim tirk'du ch'eilim;
G'vaot kiv'nei tzon.
Milifnei adon chuli aretz;
Milifnei Elohai Ya'akov.
Hahofchi hatzur agam mayim;
Chalamish l'maiy'no mayim.

WE WASH OUR HANDS

We wash our hands for the meal and say this blessing:

בָּרוּךְ אַתָּה יְיָ אֱלֹהֵינוּ מֶלֶךְ הָעוֹלָם אֲשֶׁר קִדְּשָׁנוּ בְּמִצְוֹתָיו וְצִוָּנוּ עַל נְטִילַת יָדָיִם.

Baruch Atah Adonai Eloheinu Melech ha'olam, asher kid'shanu b'mitzvotav v'tzivanu al n'tilat yadayim.

We praise You, Adonai our God, Ruler of the Universe, Who has made us holy by Your mitzvot and commands us to wash our hands.

WE SAY BLESSINGS FOR MATZAH

(Distribute pieces of the upper and middle matzah)

בָּרוּךְ אַתָּה יְיָ אֱלֹהֵינוּ מֶלֶךְ הָעוֹלָם הַמּוֹצִיא לֶחֶם מִן הָאָרֶץ.

Baruch Atah Adonai Eloheinu melech ha'olam, hamotzi lechem min ha'aretz.

We praise You, Adonai our God, Ruler of the Universe, Who brings forth bread from the earth.

בָּרוּךְ אַתָּה יְיָ אֱלֹהֵינוּ מֶלֶךְ הָעוֹלָם אֲשֶׁר קִדְּשָׁנוּ בְּמִצְוֹתָיו וְצִוָּנוּ עַל אֲכִילַת מַצָּה.

Baruch Atah Adonai Eloheinu melech ha'olam, asher kid'shanu b'mitzvotav v'tzivanu al achilat matzah.

We praise You, Adonai our God, Ruler of the Universe, Who makes us holy by Your mitzvot and commands us to eat matzah.

(Eat the matzah)

A PRAYER FOR EATING CHAMETZ

During Passover in 1944, there was no matzah at the Bergen-Belsen concentration camp, but the rabbis would not allow the inmates to endanger their lives by fasting. They decreed that chametz could be eaten, provided the following prayer be recited before meals:

Our Father in Heaven, behold it is evident and known to Thee that it is our desire to do Thy will and to celebrate the festival of Passover by eating matzah and by observing the prohibition of leavened food. But our heart is pained that the enslavement prevents us and we are in danger of our lives. Behold, we are prepared and ready to fulfill Thy commandment: "And ye shall live by [my commandments] and not die by them."

We pray to Thee that Thou mayest keep us alive and preserve us and redeem us speedily so that we may observe Thy statutes and do Thy will and serve Thee with a perfect heart. Amen.[17]

WE SAY
THE BLESSING
FOR MAROR

(Give everyone a piece of maror and some charoset)

We dip the maror into charoset to recall that our ancestors were able to withstand the bitterness of slavery, because it was sweetened by the hope of freedom.

בָּרוּךְ אַתָּה יְיָ אֱלֹהֵינוּ מֶלֶךְ הָעוֹלָם אֲשֶׁר קִדְּשָׁנוּ בְּמִצְוֹתָיו
וְצִוָּנוּ עַל אֲכִילַת מָרוֹר.

*Baruch Atah Adonai Eloheinu melech ha'olam, asher kid'shanu b'mitzvotav
v'tzivanu al achilat maror.*

We praise You, Adonai our God, Ruler of the Universe, Who makes us holy by Your mitzvot and commands us to eat maror.

(Eat the maror and charoset)

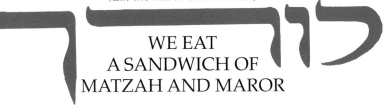

WE EAT
A SANDWICH OF
MATZAH AND MAROR

(Distribute pieces of maror and the bottom matzah)

On Passover, in the days of the Temple in Jerusalem, Rabbi Hillel would eat a sandwich made of the Pesach (lamb offering), matzah, and maror. Now we do not bring sacrifices to the Temple, so our sandwich is made only with matzah and maror.

(Eat the Hillel sandwich)

WE EAT
THE
FESTIVE MEAL

Many families traditionally serve hard-boiled eggs at the beginning of the meal, perhaps because they are a symbol of spring and renewal. They also remind us of the brave Jewish midwives who refused to carry out Pharaoh's order to kill male babies, and thus assured Jewish survival. The eggs are dipped in salt water to remember the tears of our ancestors.

 Set aside holiday storybooks to occupy children if they finish their meal before the adults (and have already prepared their afikomen ransom). You can also make a simple lotto game using the holiday symbols.

 Assign children to prepare Passover charades or trivia questions to present to the adults during dessert.

 It was customary in Eastern Europe to distribute nuts to children on Seder night to arouse their curiosity. The numerical value of the Hebrew letters in *egoz* (Hebrew for nut) is the same as that of the word *tov* (good). Here are some nut games children can play:

Left or right: Which hand is the nut in?

Odds or evens: Is there an odd or even number of nuts in someone's hand?

Nut pitching: Whoever gets the most nuts in the bowl wins.[18]

צָפוּן
WE EAT THE AFIKOMEN

After the afikomen has been found or ransomed, every-one gets a piece to eat. The afikomen is shared just as the Pesach offering was shared in the days of the Temple, to show that we are all responsible for one another. No special blessing is said because the dessert is part of the meal. We are not permitted to eat anything after the afikomen. Its taste should linger in our mouths.

בָּרֵךְ
WE SAY THE BLESSING AFTER THE MEAL

(Pour the third cup of wine and say:)

בָּרוּךְ אַתָּה יְיָ אֱלֹהֵינוּ מֶלֶךְ הָעוֹלָם, הַזָּן אֶת־הָעוֹלָם כֻּלוֹ בְּטוּבוֹ, בְּחֵן בְּחֶסֶד וּבְרַחֲמִים. הוּא נוֹתֵן לֶחֶם לְכָל־בָּשָׂר כִּי לְעוֹלָם חַסְדּוֹ. וּבְטוּבוֹ הַגָּדוֹל תָּמִיד לֹא חָסַר לָנוּ, וְאַל יֶחְסַר־לָנוּ מָזוֹן לְעוֹלָם וָעֶד בַּעֲבוּר שְׁמוֹ הַגָּדוֹל, כִּי הוּא זָן וּמְפַרְנֵס לַכֹּל וּמֵטִיב לַכֹּל וּמֵכִין מָזוֹן לְכָל־בְּרִיּוֹתָיו אֲשֶׁר בָּרָא. בָּרוּךְ אַתָּה יְיָ הַזָּן אֶת־הַכֹּל.

עוֹשֶׂה שָׁלוֹם בִּמְרוֹמָיו הוּא יַעֲשֶׂה שָׁלוֹם עָלֵינוּ וְעַל כָּל־יִשְׂרָאֵל וְאִמְרוּ אָמֵן.

We praise You, Adonai our God, Ruler of the Universe, Who in goodness, mercy, and kindness gives food to the world. Your love for us endures forever. We praise You, Adonai, Who provides food for all life.

May the Holy One, Who makes peace in the Heavens, make peace for us, for Israel, and for all the world.

Finding the afikomen can be turned into a treasure hunt. The hiders can distribute or announce clues as to its whereabouts. Or, they can sing while the searchers are looking—louder as they approach the hiding place, softer as they get farther from it.

 BIRKAT HAMAZON

Baruch Atah Adonai Eloheinu melech ha'olam, hazan et ha'olam kulo b'tuvo b'chen b'chesed uv'rachamim. Hu noten lechem l'chol basar ki l'olam chasdo. Uv'tuvo hagadol tamid lo chasar lanu v'al yech'sar lanu mazon l'olam va'ed. Ba'avur sh'mo hagadol ki hu zan um'farnes lakol umetiv lakol umechin mazon l'chol b'riyotav asher bara. Baruch Atah Adonai hazan et hakol.

Oseh shalom bimromov Hu ya'aseh shalom aleinu v'al kol Yisrael v'imru amen.

THE THIRD CUP

(Lift wine cups and say:)

בָּרוּךְ אַתָּה יְיָ אֱלֹהֵינוּ מֶלֶךְ הָעוֹלָם בּוֹרֵא פְּרִי הַגָּפֶן.

Baruch Atah Adonai Eloheinu melech ha'olam, borei p'ri hagafen.

We praise You, Adonai our God, Ruler of the Universe, Who creates the fruit of the vine.

(Drink the wine)

WELCOMING ELIJAH

(Pour a cup of wine and put it in the center of the table)

This cup is for Eliyahu Hanavi, Elijah the Prophet. We open our front door to greet our honored guest and invite him to join our seder. We pray that he will return to us bringing a time of peace and freedom.

אֵלִיָּהוּ הַנָּבִיא, אֵלִיָּהוּ הַתִּשְׁבִּי,
אֵלִיָּהוּ, אֵלִיָּהוּ, אֵלִיָּהוּ הַגִּלְעָדִי,
בִּמְהֵרָה בְיָמֵינוּ יָבֹא אֵלֵינוּ עִם מָשִׁיחַ בֶּן דָּוִד.

Eliyahu hanavi, Eliyahu haTishbi,
Eliyahu, Eliyahu, Eliyahu haGiladi,
Bimhera v'yameinu, yavo eleinu im Mashiach ben David.

May Elijah the Prophet come to us quickly and in our day, bringing the time of the Messiah.

WELCOMING MIRIAM

Miriam's Cup is a new ritual object that is placed on the seder table beside the Cup of Elijah. It is filled with water to serve as a symbol of Miriam's Well, which was the source of water for the Israelites in the desert. There are several ways to incorporate this new tradition into your seder. Some families pass around Elijah's Cup and let each person pour wine into it. This is to show that we must act together to bring about peace.[19] Similarly, some pass around Miriam's Cup, allowing each person to add water. Or you can fill Miriam's Cup and place it in the center of the table.

(Raise Miriam's Cup and say:)

Miriam's Cup represents the living waters that sustained the Jewish people after they left Egypt. According to Midrash, as a reward for Miriam's wisdom and caring, God provided a moving well of water which followed the people throughout their wanderings in the desert. Miriam's Well was said to have healing powers that refreshed their bodies and renewed their souls. We look to Miriam to guide us on our journey to repair the world.

Miriam the prophet,
Dance with us to repair the world.
Bring us soon your healing waters.[20]

49

WE SING
SONGS
OF PRAISE

יְיָ זְכָרָנוּ יְבָרֵךְ

יְבָרֵךְ אֶת־בֵּית יִשְׂרָאֵל   יְבָרֵךְ אֶת־בֵּית אַהֲרֹן.

יְבָרֵךְ יִרְאֵי יְיָ   הַקְּטַנִּים עִם הַגְּדוֹלִים.

יֹסֵף יְיָ עֲלֵיכֶם   עֲלֵיכֶם וְעַל בְּנֵיכֶם.

בְּרוּכִים אַתֶּם לַייָ   עֹשֵׂה שָׁמַיִם וָאָרֶץ.

הַשָּׁמַיִם שָׁמַיִם לַייָ   וְהָאָרֶץ נָתַן לִבְנֵי אָדָם.

לֹא הַמֵּתִים יְהַלְלוּ־יָהּ   וְלֹא כָּל־יֹרְדֵי דוּמָה.

וַאֲנַחְנוּ נְבָרֵךְ יָהּ   מֵעַתָּה וְעַד עוֹלָם,

הַלְלוּיָהּ.

הַלְלוּ אֶת־יְיָ כָּל־גּוֹיִם,   שַׁבְּחוּהוּ כָּל־הָאֻמִּים.

כִּי גָבַר עָלֵינוּ חַסְדּוֹ,   וֶאֱמֶת יְיָ לְעוֹלָם.

הַלְלוּיָהּ.

הוֹדוּ לַייָ כִּי־טוֹב   כִּי לְעוֹלָם חַסְדּוֹ.

יֹאמַר־נָא יִשְׂרָאֵל   כִּי לְעוֹלָם חַסְדּוֹ.

יֹאמְרוּ נָא בֵית אַהֲרֹן   כִּי לְעוֹלָם חַסְדּוֹ.

יֹאמְרוּ נָא יִרְאֵי יְיָ   כִּי לְעוֹלָם חַסְדּוֹ.

אֵלִי אַתָּה וְאוֹדֶךָּ   אֱלֹהַי אֲרוֹמְמֶךָּ.

הוֹדוּ לַייָ כִּי טוֹב   כִּי לְעוֹלָם חַסְדּוֹ.

Praise Adonai all nations and people, for the Holy One's
love for us is great and forever.

HALLEL ▬▬▬▬▬▬▬

Adonai z'charanu y'varech
Y'varech et bet Yisrael
Y'varech et bet Aharon.
Y'varech yir'ei Adonai
Hak'tanim im hag'dolim.
Yosef Adonai Aleichem
Aleichem v'al b'neichem.
B'ruchim atem l'Adonai
Oseh shamayim va'aretz.
Hashamayim shamayim l'Adonai
V'ha'aretz natan liv'nei adam.
Lo hametim y'hallelu-Ya
V'lo kol yor'dei dumah.
Va'anachnu n'varech Ya
Me'atah v'ad olam, halleluyah.

Hallelu et Adonai kol goyim
Shabchuhu kol ha'umim.
Ki gavar aleinu chasdo
V'emet Adonai l'olam halleluyah.

Hodu l'Adonai ki tov ki l'olam chasdo.
Yomar-na Yisrael ki l'olam chasdo.
Yomru-na vet Aharon ki l'olam chasdo.
Yomru-na yir'ei Adonai ki l'olam chasdo.

Eli Atah v'odeka Elohai aromemeka.
Hodu l'Adonai ki tov ki l'olam chasdo.

WE COUNT THE OMER

(Second night only)

Jewish holidays celebrate important historical moments, and many are also linked to the seasons of nature. In addition to celebrating our going out of Egypt, Passover marks the beginning of the barley harvest. On the second day of Passover, an *omer*, a sheaf of barley, was brought to the Temple as an offering. Shavuot, which comes 49 days later, commemorates the giving of the Torah, and also marks the beginning of the wheat harvest. At the second seder it is traditional to begin counting off these 49 days, referred to as the Days of the Omer.

This symbolic "countdown" from Pesach to Shavuot shows the connection between the two holidays. Our freedom from slavery was not complete until we received the Torah, which gives our lives purpose and meaning. We count the Omer with a blessing:

בָּרוּךְ אַתָּה יְיָ אֱלֹהֵינוּ מֶלֶךְ הָעוֹלָם אֲשֶׁר קִדְּשָׁנוּ בְּמִצְוֹתָיו וְצִוָּנוּ עַל סְפִירַת הָעֹמֶר.

הַיּוֹם יוֹם אֶחָד לָעֹמֶר.

Baruch Atah Adonai Eloheinu melech ha'olam, asher kid'shanu b'mitzvotav v'tzivanu al s'firat ha'omer. Hayom yom echad la'omer.

We praise You, Adonai our God, Ruler of the Universe, who makes us holy by Your mitzvot and commands us to count the Omer.

Today is the First Day of the Omer.

The days from Pesach to Shavuot were an anxious time in ancient Israel, for all wondered if the wheat harvest would be plentiful. How are our economic worries both the same and different from those of the ancient Israelites?

 Have children make an Omer Tzedakah box. Each night (except for Shabbat and holidays), as the day of the Omer is counted, a family member can drop a coin in the box. After Shavuot, the money may be donated to a charity that provides food for the needy.[21]

SEDER SONGS

אַדִּיר הוּא

אַדִּיר הוּא, אַדִּיר הוּא, יִבְנֶה בֵיתוֹ בְּקָרוֹב, בִּמְהֵרָה בִּמְהֵרָה, בְּיָמֵינוּ בְּקָרוֹב. אֵל בְּנֵה, אֵל בְּנֵה, בְּנֵה בֵיתְךָ בְּקָרוֹב.

בָּחוּר הוּא, גָּדוֹל הוּא, דָּגוּל הוּא, יִבְנֶה בֵיתוֹ בְּקָרוֹב, בִּמְהֵרָה בִּמְהֵרָה, בְּיָמֵינוּ בְּקָרוֹב. אֵל בְּנֵה, אֵל בְּנֵה, בְּנֵה בֵיתְךָ בְּקָרוֹב.

הָדוּר הוּא, וָתִיק הוּא, זַכַּאי הוּא, חָסִיד הוּא, יִבְנֶה בֵיתוֹ בְּקָרוֹב, בִּמְהֵרָה בִּמְהֵרָה, בְּיָמֵינוּ בְּקָרוֹב. אֵל בְּנֵה, אֵל בְּנֵה, בְּנֵה בֵיתְךָ בְּקָרוֹב.

טָהוֹר הוּא, יָחִיד הוּא, כַּבִּיר הוּא, לָמוּד הוּא, מֶלֶךְ הוּא, נוֹרָא הוּא, סַגִּיב הוּא, עִזּוּז הוּא, פּוֹדֶה הוּא, צַדִּיק הוּא, יִבְנֶה בֵיתוֹ בְּקָרוֹב, בִּמְהֵרָה בִּמְהֵרָה, בְּיָמֵינוּ בְּקָרוֹב. אֵל בְּנֵה, אֵל בְּנֵה, בְּנֵה בֵיתְךָ בְּקָרוֹב.

קָדוֹשׁ הוּא, רַחוּם הוּא, שַׁדַּי הוּא, תַּקִּיף הוּא, יִבְנֶה בֵיתוֹ בְּקָרוֹב, בִּמְהֵרָה בִּמְהֵרָה, בְּיָמֵינוּ בְּקָרוֹב. אֵל בְּנֵה, אֵל בְּנֵה, בְּנֵה בֵיתְךָ בְּקָרוֹב.

Mighty is God.

May Adonai's kingdom be established speedily and in our days.

God is first, great, exalted.

God is glorious, faithful, righteous, gracious.

God is pure, unique, mighty, wise, majestic, awesome, splendid, strong, redeeming, righteous.

God is holy, compassionate, almighty, and powerful.

The song *Adir Hu* lists the attributes of God in alphabetical order in Hebrew. Compose a version that describes God that follows the English alphabet.

 ADIR HU

Adir Hu, Adir Hu
Yivneh veito b'karov.
Bimherah, bimherah
B'yamenu b'karov.
El b'nai El b'nai
B'nai veitcha b'karov.

Bachur Hu, Gadol Hu, Dagul Hu...

Hadur Hu, Vatik Hu, Zakkai Hu, Chassid Hu ...

Tahor Hu, Yachid Hu, Kabir Hu, Lamud Hu,
Melech Hu, Norah Hu, Saggiv Hu, Izzuz Hu,
Podeh Hu, Tzaddik Hu ...

Kadosh Hu, Rachum Hu, Shaddai Hu, Takif Hu ...

אֶחָד מִי יוֹדֵעַ

אֶחָד מִי יוֹדֵעַ? אֶחָד אֲנִי יוֹדֵעַ: אֶחָד אֱלֹהֵינוּ שֶׁבַּשָּׁמַיִם וּבָאָרֶץ.

שְׁנַיִם מִי יוֹדֵעַ? שְׁנַיִם אֲנִי יוֹדֵעַ: שְׁנֵי לֻחוֹת הַבְּרִית, אֶחָד אֱלֹהֵינוּ שֶׁבַּשָּׁמַיִם וּבָאָרֶץ.

שְׁלוֹשָׁה מִי יוֹדֵעַ? שְׁלוֹשָׁה אֲנִי יוֹדֵעַ: שְׁלוֹשָׁה אָבוֹת, שְׁנֵי לֻחוֹת הַבְּרִית, אֶחָד אֱלֹהֵינוּ שֶׁבַּשָּׁמַיִם וּבָאָרֶץ.

אַרְבַּע מִי יוֹדֵעַ? אַרְבַּע אֲנִי יוֹדֵעַ: אַרְבַּע אִמָּהוֹת, שְׁלוֹשָׁה אָבוֹת, שְׁנֵי לֻחוֹת הַבְּרִית, אֶחָד אֱלֹהֵינוּ שֶׁבַּשָּׁמַיִם וּבָאָרֶץ.

חֲמִשָּׁה מִי יוֹדֵעַ? חֲמִשָּׁה אֲנִי יוֹדֵעַ: חֲמִשָּׁה חֻמְשֵׁי תוֹרָה, אַרְבַּע אִמָּהוֹת, שְׁלוֹשָׁה אָבוֹת, שְׁנֵי לֻחוֹת הַבְּרִית, אֶחָד אֱלֹהֵינוּ שֶׁבַּשָּׁמַיִם וּבָאָרֶץ.

שִׁשָּׁה מִי יוֹדֵעַ? שִׁשָּׁה אֲנִי יוֹדֵעַ: שִׁשָּׁה סִדְרֵי מִשְׁנָה, חֲמִשָּׁה חֻמְשֵׁי תוֹרָה, אַרְבַּע אִמָּהוֹת, שְׁלוֹשָׁה אָבוֹת, שְׁנֵי לֻחוֹת הַבְּרִית, אֶחָד אֱלֹהֵינוּ שֶׁבַּשָּׁמַיִם וּבָאָרֶץ.

שִׁבְעָה מִי יוֹדֵעַ? שִׁבְעָה אֲנִי יוֹדֵעַ: שִׁבְעָה יְמֵי שַׁבַּתָּא, שִׁשָּׁה סִדְרֵי מִשְׁנָה, חֲמִשָּׁה חֻמְשֵׁי תוֹרָה, אַרְבַּע אִמָּהוֹת, שְׁלוֹשָׁה אָבוֹת, שְׁנֵי לֻחוֹת הַבְּרִית, אֶחָד אֱלֹהֵינוּ שֶׁבַּשָּׁמַיִם וּבָאָרֶץ.

שְׁמוֹנָה מִי יוֹדֵעַ? שְׁמוֹנָה אֲנִי יוֹדֵעַ: שְׁמוֹנָה יְמֵי מִילָה, שִׁבְעָה יְמֵי שַׁבַּתָּא, שִׁשָּׁה סִדְרֵי מִשְׁנָה, חֲמִשָּׁה חֻמְשֵׁי תוֹרָה, אַרְבַּע אִמָּהוֹת, שְׁלוֹשָׁה אָבוֹת, שְׁנֵי לֻחוֹת הַבְּרִית, אֶחָד אֱלֹהֵינוּ שֶׁבַּשָּׁמַיִם וּבָאָרֶץ.

תִּשְׁעָה מִי יוֹדֵעַ? תִּשְׁעָה אֲנִי יוֹדֵעַ: תִּשְׁעָה יַרְחֵי לֵדָה, שְׁמוֹנָה יְמֵי מִילָה, שִׁבְעָה יְמֵי שַׁבַּתָּא, שִׁשָּׁה סִדְרֵי מִשְׁנָה, חֲמִשָּׁה חֻמְשֵׁי תוֹרָה, אַרְבַּע אִמָּהוֹת, שְׁלוֹשָׁה אָבוֹת, שְׁנֵי לֻחוֹת הַבְּרִית, אֶחָד אֱלֹהֵינוּ שֶׁבַּשָּׁמַיִם וּבָאָרֶץ.

עֲשָׂרָה מִי יוֹדֵעַ? עֲשָׂרָה אֲנִי יוֹדֵעַ: עֲשָׂרָה דִבְּרַיָּא, תִּשְׁעָה יַרְחֵי לֵדָה, שְׁמוֹנָה יְמֵי מִילָה, שִׁבְעָה יְמֵי שַׁבַּתָּא, שִׁשָּׁה סִדְרֵי מִשְׁנָה, חֲמִשָּׁה חֻמְשֵׁי תוֹרָה, אַרְבַּע אִמָּהוֹת, שְׁלוֹשָׁה אָבוֹת, שְׁנֵי לֻחוֹת הַבְּרִית, אֶחָד אֱלֹהֵינוּ שֶׁבַּשָּׁמַיִם וּבָאָרֶץ.

אַחַד עָשָׂר מִי יוֹדֵעַ? אַחַד עָשָׂר אֲנִי יוֹדֵעַ: אַחַד עָשָׂר כּוֹכְבַיָּא, עֲשָׂרָה דִבְּרַיָּא, תִּשְׁעָה יַרְחֵי לֵדָה, שְׁמוֹנָה יְמֵי מִילָה, שִׁבְעָה יְמֵי שַׁבַּתָּא, שִׁשָּׁה סִדְרֵי מִשְׁנָה, חֲמִשָּׁה חֻמְשֵׁי תוֹרָה, אַרְבַּע אִמָּהוֹת, שְׁלוֹשָׁה אָבוֹת, שְׁנֵי לֻחוֹת הַבְּרִית, אֶחָד אֱלֹהֵינוּ שֶׁבַּשָּׁמַיִם וּבָאָרֶץ.

שְׁנֵים עָשָׂר מִי יוֹדֵעַ? שְׁנֵים עָשָׂר אֲנִי יוֹדֵעַ: שְׁנֵים עָשָׂר שִׁבְטַיָּא, אַחַד עָשָׂר כּוֹכְבַיָּא, עֲשָׂרָה דִבְּרַיָּא, תִּשְׁעָה יַרְחֵי לֵדָה, שְׁמוֹנָה יְמֵי מִילָה, שִׁבְעָה יְמֵי שַׁבַּתָּא, שִׁשָּׁה סִדְרֵי מִשְׁנָה, חֲמִשָּׁה חֻמְשֵׁי תוֹרָה, אַרְבַּע אִמָּהוֹת, שְׁלוֹשָׁה אָבוֹת, שְׁנֵי לֻחוֹת הַבְּרִית, אֶחָד אֱלֹהֵינוּ שֶׁבַּשָּׁמַיִם וּבָאָרֶץ.

שְׁלוֹשָׁה עָשָׂר מִי יוֹדֵעַ? שְׁלוֹשָׁה עָשָׂר אֲנִי יוֹדֵעַ: שְׁלוֹשָׁה עָשָׂר מִדַּיָּא, שְׁנֵים עָשָׂר שִׁבְטַיָּא, אַחַד עָשָׂר כּוֹכְבַיָּא, עֲשָׂרָה דִבְּרַיָּא, תִּשְׁעָה יַרְחֵי לֵדָה, שְׁמוֹנָה יְמֵי מִילָה, שִׁבְעָה יְמֵי שַׁבַּתָּא, שִׁשָּׁה סִדְרֵי מִשְׁנָה, חֲמִשָּׁה חֻמְשֵׁי תוֹרָה, אַרְבַּע אִמָּהוֹת, שְׁלוֹשָׁה אָבוֹת, שְׁנֵי לֻחוֹת הַבְּרִית, אֶחָד אֱלֹהֵינוּ שֶׁבַּשָּׁמַיִם וּבָאָרֶץ.

ECHAD MI YODEA ▬▬▬▬▬▬

Echad mi yodea?
Echad ani yodea.
Echad Eloheinu shebashamayim uva'aretz.

Shnei luchot habrit . . .
Shloshah avot . . .
Arba imahot . . .
Chamishah chumshei Torah . . .
Shishah sidrei Mishnah . . .
Shiv'ah y'mei shabbata . . .
Shmonah y'mei milah . . .
Tishah yarchei leidah . . .
Asarah debraya . . .
Achad asar kochvaya . . .
Shnem asar shivtaya . . .
Shloshah asar midaya . . .

Who know ONE? I know ONE.
One is our God Who is in heaven and earth.
Two are the two tablets of the law.
Three are the three fathers.
Four are the four mothers.
Five are the five books of the Torah.
Six are the six books of the Mishnah.
Seven are the seven days of the week.
Eight are the eight days until circumcision.
Nine are the nine months of pregnancy.
Ten are the Ten Commandments.
Eleven are the eleven stars in Joseph's dream.
Twelve are the Twelve Tribes of Israel.
Thirteen are the thirteen attributes of God.

Numbers are important symbols in Jewish
tradition. For example:

> 13 is Bar/Bat Mitzvah
> 2 are the loaves of challah on Shabbat
> 3 are the angels who visited Abraham
> Can you think of others?

 Be prepared to identify:
> the three fathers,
> the four mothers,
> the five books of the Torah,
> the six books of the Mishnah,
> the twelve tribes of Israel.

חַד גַּדְיָא

חַד גַּדְיָא, חַד גַּדְיָא, דְּזַבֵּן
אַבָּא בִּתְרֵי זוּזֵי, חַד גַּדְיָא,
חַד גַּדְיָא.

וְאָתָא שׁוּנְרָא וְאָכַל לְגַדְיָא,
דְּזַבֵּן אַבָּא בִּתְרֵי זוּזֵי, חַד
גַּדְיָא, חַד גַּדְיָא.

וְאָתָא כַלְבָּא וְנָשַׁךְ לְשׁוּנְרָא,
דְּאָכַל לְגַדְיָא, דְּזַבֵּן אַבָּא
בִּתְרֵי זוּזֵי, חַד גַּדְיָא, חַד
גַּדְיָא.

וְאָתָא חוּטְרָא וְהִכָּה
לְכַלְבָּא, דְּנָשַׁךְ לְשׁוּנְרָא,
דְּאָכַל לְגַדְיָא, דְּזַבֵּן אַבָּא
בִּתְרֵי זוּזֵי, חַד גַּדְיָא, חַד
גַּדְיָא.

וְאָתָא נוּרָא וְשָׂרַף לְחוּטְרָא,
דְּהִכָּה לְכַלְבָּא, דְּנָשַׁךְ
לְשׁוּנְרָא, דְּאָכַל לְגַדְיָא, דְּזַבֵּן
אַבָּא בִּתְרֵי זוּזֵי, חַד גַּדְיָא,
חַד גַּדְיָא.

וְאָתָא מַיָּא וְכָבָה לְנוּרָא,
דְּשָׂרַף לְחוּטְרָא, דְּהִכָּה
לְכַלְבָּא, דְּנָשַׁךְ לְשׁוּנְרָא,
דְּאָכַל לְגַדְיָא, דְּזַבֵּן אַבָּא
בִּתְרֵי זוּזֵי, חַד גַּדְיָא, חַד
גַּדְיָא.

וְאָתָא תוֹרָא וְשָׁתָא לְמַיָּא,
דְּכָבָה לְנוּרָא, דְּשָׂרַף

לְחוּטְרָא, דְּהִכָּה לְכַלְבָּא,
דְּנָשַׁךְ לְשׁוּנְרָא, דְּאָכַל
לְגַדְיָא, דְּזַבֵּן אַבָּא בִּתְרֵי זוּזֵי,
חַד גַּדְיָא, חַד גַּדְיָא.

וְאָתָא הַשּׁוֹחֵט וְשָׁחַט
לְתוֹרָא, דְּשָׁתָה לְמַיָּא, דְּכָבָה
לְנוּרָא, דְּשָׂרַף לְחוּטְרָא,
דְּהִכָּה לְכַלְבָּא, דְּנָשַׁךְ
לְשׁוּנְרָא, דְּאָכַל לְגַדְיָא, דְּזַבֵּן
אַבָּא בִּתְרֵי זוּזֵי, חַד גַּדְיָא,
חַד גַּדְיָא.

וְאָתָא מַלְאַךְ הַמָּוֶת, וְשָׁחַט
לַשּׁוֹחֵט, דְּשָׁחַט לְתוֹרָא,
דְּשָׁתָה לְמַיָּא, דְּכָבָה לְנוּרָא,
דְּשָׂרַף לְחוּטְרָא, דְּהִכָּה
לְכַלְבָּא, דְּנָשַׁךְ לְשׁוּנְרָא,
דְּאָכַל לְגַדְיָא, דְּזַבֵּן אַבָּא
בִּתְרֵי זוּזֵי, חַד גַּדְיָא, חַד
גַּדְיָא.

וְאָתָא הַקָּדוֹשׁ בָּרוּךְ הוּא,
וְשָׁחַט לְמַלְאַךְ הַמָּוֶת,
דְּשָׁחַט לַשּׁוֹחֵט, דְּשָׁחַט
לְתוֹרָא, דְּשָׁתָה לְמַיָּא, דְּכָבָה
לְנוּרָא, דְּשָׂרַף לְחוּטְרָא,
דְּהִכָּה לְכַלְבָּא, דְּנָשַׁךְ
לְשׁוּנְרָא, דְּאָכַל לְגַדְיָא, דְּזַבֵּן
אַבָּא בִּתְרֵי זוּזֵי, חַד גַּדְיָא,
חַד גַּדְיָא.

CHAD GADYA

Chad gadya, chad gadya.
Dizvan aba bit'rei zuzei
Chad gadya, chad gadya.

V'ata shunra v'achal l'gadya
Dizvan aba bit'rei zuzei
Chad gadya, chad gadya.

V'ata chalba v'nashach l'shunra . . .
V'ata chutra v'hika l'chalba . . .
V'ata nura v'saraf l'chutra . . .
V'ata maya v'chava l'nura . . .
V'ata tora v'shata l'maya . . .
V'ata hashochet v'shachat l'tora . . .
V'ata Malach Hamavet v'shachat l'shochet . . .
V'ata Hakadosh Baruch Hu v'shachat l'Malach
Hamavet . . .

One little goat, one little goat
That my father bought for two zuzim.
One little goat, one little goat.
Along came a cat and ate the goat . . .
Along came a dog and bit the cat . . .
Along came a stick and beat the dog . . .
Along came a fire and burnt the stick . . .
Along came water and put out the fire . . .
Along came an ox and drank the water . . .
Along came a butcher and slaughtered the ox . . .
Along came the Angel of Death and killed the butcher . . .
Along came the Holy One and slew the Angel of Death.

 Make cut-outs or puppets to use during the
singing of Chad Gadya.

 Chad Gadya is an allegory describing Israel's history. The kid is Israel, purchased
with two zuzim, the two tablets of the law.
Next is a list of Israel's oppressors: the cat
is Assyria, the dog—Babylonia, the stick—
Persia, fire—Greece, water—Rome, the
ox—Saracens, the butcher—the Crusaders,
the Angel of Death—the Ottomans. But the
song ends with an expression of hope that
the Holy One will bring peace and eternal
life to the people of Israel.

WE COMPLETE THE SEDER

THE FOURTH CUP

(Lift wine cups and say:)

בָּרוּךְ אַתָּה יְיָ אֱלֹהֵינוּ מֶלֶךְ הָעוֹלָם בּוֹרֵא פְּרִי הַגָּפֶן.

Baruch Atah Adonai Eloheinu melech ha'olam, borei p'ri hagafen.

We praise You, Adonai our God, Ruler of the Universe,
Who creates the fruit of the vine.

(Drink the wine)

Chasal siddur Pesach k'hilchato,
K'chol mishpato v'chukato.
Ka'asher zachinu l'sader oto
Ken nizkeh la'asoto.
Zach shochen m'onah
Komem k'hal adat mi manah.
B'karov nahel nitei chanah
P'duyim l'Zion b'rina.

חֲסַל סִדּוּר פֶּסַח כְּהִלְכָתוֹ,
כְּכָל־מִשְׁפָּטוֹ וְחֻקָּתוֹ.
כַּאֲשֶׁר זָכִינוּ לְסַדֵּר אוֹתוֹ,
כֵּן נִזְכֶּה לַעֲשׂוֹתוֹ.
זָךְ שׁוֹכֵן מְעוֹנָה,
קוֹמֵם קְהַל עֲדַת מִי מָנָה.
בְּקָרוֹב נַהֵל נִטְעֵי כַנָּה,
פְּדוּיִים לְצִיּוֹן בְּרִנָּה.

Our seder is now completed.
May our service be acceptable to You, Adonai our God,
And may we be granted the blessing
Of celebrating Pesach for many years to come.
Pure and Holy One, dwelling on high,
Raise up your people with love
And lead us to Zion in joyful song.[22]

לַשָּׁנָה הַבָּאָה בִּירוּשָׁלָיִם.

Lashanah haba'ah b'Yerushalayim!

NEXT YEAR IN JERUSALEM!

THE FIFTH CUP

Some families drink a fifth cup of wine in gratitude for the State of Israel. You may wish to do this before concluding the seder.

 HATIKVAH

כָּל עוֹד בַּלֵּבָב פְּנִימָה נֶפֶשׁ יְהוּדִי הוֹמִיָּה,
וּלְפַאֲתֵי מִזְרָח קָדִימָה עַיִן לְצִיּוֹן צוֹפִיָּה.
עוֹד לֹא אָבְדָה תִקְוָתֵנוּ הַתִּקְוָה בַּת שְׁנוֹת אַלְפַּיִם,
לִהְיוֹת עַם חָפְשִׁי בְּאַרְצֵנוּ אֶרֶץ צִיּוֹן וִירוּשָׁלָיִם.

Kol od balevav p'nimah,
Nefesh Yehudi homiya.
Ul'fatei mizrach kadimah
Ayin l'tzion tzofiyah.
Od lo avdah tikvatenu,
Hatikvah, bat shnot alpayim,
Li'yot am chofshi b'artzenu
Eretz Tzion v'Yerushalyim.[23]

The heart and soul of the Jew echoes the ancient hope to be a free people in the land of Zion.

FREEDOM SONGS

GO TELL IT ON THE MOUNTAIN

Go tell it on the mountain,
Over the hills and everywhere.
Go tell it on the mountain—
Let my people go!
Who are the people dressed in white?
Let my people go!
Must be the children of the Israelites—
Let my people go!
Who are the people dressed in red?
Let my people go!
Must be the people that Moses led—
Let my people go!
Add your own verses!

MOSES

There is a man come into Egypt,
And Moses is his name.
When he saw the grief upon us,
In his heart there burned a flame.
In his heart there burned a flame, O Lord,
I his heart there burned a flame.
When he saw the grief upon us,
In his heart there burned a flame.

LET MY PEOPLE GO

When Israel was in Egypt land.
Let my people go.
Oppressed so hard they could not stand.
Let my people go.
Go down, Moses, way down in Egypt land.
Tell ol' Pharaoh to let my people go.
"Thus saith the Lord," bold Moses said.
"Let my people go.
"If not I'll smite your first-born dead.
"Let my people go."
Go down, Moses, way down in Egypt land.
Tell ol' Pharaoh to let my people go.

NOTES

1. These ideas are from "Developing Jewish Rituals For Your Family," by Shoshana Silberman in *The Jewish Family Book*, Sharon Strassfeld and Kathy Green, eds. New York: Bantam, 1981, p.75.

2. Susannah Heschel suggested placing an orange on the seder plate as a symbol of inclusion. See myjewishlearning.com or ritualwell.org.

3. This custom was taught to us by Katie and Bob Zimring who joined our family for several sedarim. It is further explained in "A Passover Haggadah" by Michael Strassfeld, ed. *Conservative Judaism*, Vol. XXXII, Number 3, Spring 1979, p.6.

4. This explanation is found in Michael Strassfeld, *A Passover Haggadah*, p.8.

5. I learned this custom from Rabbi Jeffrey Schein.

6. The idea for this activity is based on a discussion of The Four Children in "The Rainbow Seder" by Arthur Waskow in *The Shalom Seders*, New Jewish Agenda. New York: Adama Books, pp.36-37.

7. This activity was suggested by Rabbi Jeffrey Schein.

8. From *Passover Music Box*, words and music by Shirley R. Cohen ©1951 Kinor Records.

9. This activity is based on a lesson taught by Amy Kassiola.

10. *Exodus Rabbah, 3.*

11. *Passover Music Box.*

12. *Passover Music Box.*

13. I learned this from Audrey Friedman Marcus at a workshop at Gratz College.

14. This is based on an activity in Michael Strassfeld, *A Passover Haggadah*, p. 8.

15. A discussion of Pesach, maror, and matzah as symbols of courage is found in *The Passover Haggadah*, Rabbi Shlomo Riskin, ed., New York: Ktav, 1983, pp. 102–104.

16. The idea of using similes to teach about God and prayer was taught to me by Dr. Ellen Charry.

17. A copy of the original handwritten prayer is at the Ghetto Fighters House in Israel.

18. The nut games are described in *The Passover Anthology*, by Philip Goodman. Philadelphia: Jewish Publication Society, 1966, pp. 407–408.

19. This explanation is found in Michael Strassfeld, *A Passover Haggadah*, p. 72.

20. Shoshana Silberman. *The Jewish World Family Haggadah*. IBooks: 2005.

21. I learned this tzedakah idea from Rob Agus at an inter-chavurah retreat.

22. The idea of placing *Nirtzah* at the very end of the seder, after the table songs, is from Michael Strassfeld, *A Passover Haggadah*.

23. *Hatikvah* by Naftali Imber.

Dr. Shoshana Silberman is a Consultant at the Auerbach Central Agency for Jewish Education in Philadelphia. She also conducts workshops across North America. Formerly, she was a teacher and Jewish school principal. Shoshana is the author of: *The Family Haggadah I & II* (Kar-Ben), *The Whole Megillah (Almost!)* (Kar-Ben), *Tiku Shofar: A Mahzor for Children and Their Parents* (United Synagogue), *Siddur Shema Yisrael: A Siddur for Sabbath and Festivals for Students and Families* (United Synagogue), *Student Game Book for Hebrew and Prayer* (Behrman House), *Family Rhymes for Jewish Times* (United Synagogue), *The Jewish World Family Haggadah* (ibooks/ Brick Tower Press,) and *Active Jewish Learning* (Torah Aura).

Katherine Janus Kahn, an illustrator, calligrapher, and sculptor, studied Fine Arts at the Bezalel School in Jerusalem and the University of Iowa. She has illustrated an impressive list of books including the acclaimed *Sammy Spider* series, a set of Family Services for Shabbat and the holidays, and many other award-winning story, activity and board books for young children. She lives in Wheaton, MD with her husband David.